OCEAN

LIFE CYCLES

Sean Callery

Consultant: David Burnie

KINGFISHER

First published 2011 by Kingfisher
This edition published 2012 by Kingfisher
an imprint of Macmillan Children's Books
a division of Macmillan Publishers Limited
20 New Wharf Road, London N1 9RR
Basingstoke and Oxford
Associated companies throughout the world
www.panmacmillan.com

ISBN 978-0-7534-3459-8

1 3 5 7 9 8 6 4 2
1TR/0412/WKT/UNTD/140MA

A CIP catalogue record for this book is available from the British Library.

Printed in China

Note to readers: the website addresses listed in this book are correct at
the time of going to print. However, due to the ever-changing nature
of the internet, website addresses and content can change. Websites
can contain links that are unsuitable for children. The publisher cannot
be held responsible for changes in website addresses or content, or for
information obtained through a third party. We strongly advise that
internet searches be supervised by an adult.

The publisher would like to thank the following for permission to reproduce their material. Every care has been taken to trace copyright holders. However, if there have been unintentional omissions or failure to trace copyright holders, we apologise and will, if informed, endeavour to make corrections in any future edition.
Top = t; Bottom = b; Centre = c; Left = l; Right = r

All artwork Stuart Jackson-Carter (Peter Kavanagh Art Agency)

Cover c Shutterstock/idreamphoto; cover b Shutterstock/Igor Kovalchuk; cover tl Photolibrary/Peter Arnold Images; cover tcl Naturepl/Wild Wonders of Europe; cover tcr Photolibrary/Animals Animals; cover tr Getty/NGS; back cover Shutterstock/Rich Carey. Page 1 Shutterstock/Calek; 2 Alamy/Premier; 4tr Shutterstock/cbpix; 4bl Naturepl/Andy Rouse; 5tl Shutterstock/Sandy Maya Matzen; 5br Seapics/James D. Watt; 6bl Bluegreenpictures/David Fleetham; 6tr Frank Lane Picture Agency (FLPA)/David Bavendam/Minden; 6br Photolibrary/OSF; 7tl Photolibrary/Waterframe; 7bl Photolibrary/Bios; 7tcr Shutterstock/Rui Manuel Teles Gomes; 7tr Shutterstock/frantisekhojdysz; 7ctr FLPA/Chris Newbert/Minden; 7cr FLPA/Hans Leijnse/Minden; 7cbr Photolibrary/Robert Harding; 7cb Shutterstock/Studio 37; 7br Shutterstock/oilas32; 8bl Shutterstock/Mark Doherty; 8blc Getty/ Stone; 9tl Naturepl/Georgette Douwa; 9bl Alamy/Danita Delimont; 9tr Shutterstock/Joanna Zopoth-Lipiejko; 9ctr Photolibrary/Tsuneo Nakamura; 9cbr Photolibrary/OSF; 9br Shutterstock/Wallenrock; 9bc Shutterstock/Joze Maucec; 10bl iStockphoto/Boris Tarasov; 11tr Shutterstock/Milena Katzer; 11ctr Corbis/Norbert Wu; 11cr Shutterstock/Olga Khoroshunova; 11bc Shutterstock/Tatiana Belova; 11br Shutterstock/Mark William Penny; 12c Photolibrary/Waterframe; 12bl Image Quest Marine/Masa Ushiod; 13tl Photolibrary/Waterframe 13bl Photolibrary/Waterframe; 13tr Shutterstock/Vlad61; 13ctr Photolibrary/Peter Arnold Images; 13cr Photolibrary/Peter Arnold Images; 13cbr Shutterstock/Undersea Discoveries; 13bc Shutterstock/Geoffrey Lawrence; 13br Shutterstock/A Cotton Photo; 13br Shutterstock/1971yes; 14bl FLPA/Silvestris Fotoservice; 15tl Ardea/Waterframe; 15ctr Getty/NGS; 15cr Getty/NGS; 15cbr Naturepl/David Shale; 15cbr Shutterstock/omers; 15bc Shutterstock/Pavol Kmeto; 16bl Shutterstock/Studio 37; 16blc Seapics; 16br FLPA/DP Wilson; 17br FLPA/DP Wilson; 17tr Shutterstock/Vlad61; 17cr Naturepl/David Shale; 17cbr Naturepl/David Shale; 17br Shutterstock/michaeljung; 18bl Alamy/Picture Press; 18tr FLPA/Michael Durham/Minden; 18br Alamy/Danita Delimont; 19tl Alamy/Mark Conlin; 19bl Alamy/Lucidio Studio Inc; 19tr Shutterstock/Chee-Onn Leong; 19ctr Photolibrary/Alaskastock; 19cr Alamy/Mark Conlin; 19cbr Photolibrary/Alaskastock; 19br Shutterstock/bierchen; 20bl Alamy/Steve Bloom; 20tr Alamy/All Canada Photos; 20br Alamy/Christopher Zimmer; 21tl Alamy/Mira; 21bl FLPA/Suzi Eszterhas/Minden; 21tr Shutterstock/Studio 37; 21ctr Shutterstock/Eric Isselee; 21cr Shutterstock/ODM Studio; 21cbr Shutterstock/Robin Phinizy; 21br Shutterstock/Paul Clarke; 21br Shutterstock/Studio 37; 22bl Getty/NGS; 23tr Shutterstock; 23ctr Naturepl/Jurgen Freund; 23cr Getty/Roger Horrocks; 23cbr Naturepl/Jurgen Freund; 23br Shutterstock/DJ Mattaar; 24bl Seapics/Amar & Isabelle Guillen; 24tr Photolibrary/Peter Arnold Images; 24br Naturepl/Wild Wonders of Europe; 25tl Shutterstock/idreamphoto; 25bl Photolibrary/Animals Animals; 25ctr Photolibrary/Animals Animals; 25cr Naturepl/Ingo Arndt; 25cbr Photoshot/Franco Banfi/NHPA; 25bc Shutterstock/Ocean Image Photography; 25br Shutterstock/Stubblefield Photography; 26bl Photolibrary/Alaskastock; 26tr Seapics/David B. Fleetham; 26br Seapics/Lori Mazzuca; 27tl Photolibrary/All Canada Photos; 27bl Photolibrary/Animals Animals; 27tr Shutterstock/Stephan Kerkhofs; 27ctr Naturepl/Michael S. Nolan; 27cr Naturepl/Doug Perrine; 27cbr Photolibrary/Alaskastock; 27br Photolibrary/Alaskastock; 27br Shutterstock/Nikita Tiunov; 27bc Shutterstock/frantisekhojdsz

Contents

Introduction

The oceans of the world are home to millions of amazing animals, from the largest on Earth to some of the tiniest, too small for us to see with the naked eye.

All these living things have to eat to stay alive. Some make their own food using the sun's energy, some eat plants and many try to eat each other. The list of who eats who is called a food chain.

The first animal in a food chain is called a primary consumer because it eats other living things. This clownfish, for example, eats algae and other sea animals.

NORTH AMERICA

Food chain 2

Atlantic ocean

North Pacific ocean

Food chain 3

SOUTH AMERICA

South Pacific ocean

Most food chains start with things that make their own food using the sun's energy. They are known as producers and include seaweed (left) and algae, called phytoplankton, which drift in the oceans.

Next in a food chain is what is known as a secondary consumer. It might be a carnivore or an omnivore. Puffins are secondary consumers that eat fish and small sea animals.

This book takes you along three food chains from oceans in different parts of the world. You will find out about the life cycles of 11 animals: how they are born, grow, reproduce and die.

Arctic ocean

EUROPE

ASIA

AFRICA

Equator

Indian ocean

Food chain 1

AUSTRALIA

Southern ocean

At the top of a food chain is an animal like this swordfish, which has no predators because it is so fast and fierce.

ANTARCTICA

Coral

Coral reefs grow mostly in warm waters such as the tropical seas around the Equator. They are built up by tiny animals called polyps. The hard, chalky cups that the polyps grow in are left behind when they die and form the coral rock.

1 Coral polyps reproduce in two ways. The first way is by producing eggs. The females release the eggs into the water and the males fertilize them.

2 Tiny larvae hatch from the eggs and drift in the water. Soon they land on hard surfaces like rock and fix themselves there.

4 Coral polyps also reproduce by splitting in half. They split again and again until there is a whole colony of polyps.

3 The larvae grow into polyps. Their bodies are like little bags with tentacles at one end for catching prey. The polyps grow bigger until they can produce eggs themselves.

Did you know?

Corals can be all sorts of shapes. Some look like mushrooms, others look like cones or even cabbages!

Many sea animals sneak into gaps in the coral to hide from predators, or wait there to pounce on prey.

Coral reefs protect some coasts. They slow down the sea so that big waves hit the land less hard and do less damage.

Coral reefs can be hundreds or even thousands of years old, but coral polyps are eaten in huge numbers by one animal...

Crown of thorns starfish

Crown of thorns starfish eat coral. They crawl across the reef sucking up the coral polyps, and leaving dead coral rock behind them.

1 The female starfish release millions of eggs and the males fertilize them. This is called spawning.

2 The eggs develop into larvae, which drift in the water and feed on tiny plant-like algae.

4 The starfish grow more arms. After six months they are as big as your fingernail. Fully grown adults can be 35 centimetres across.

3 The larvae settle on rock, the seabed, shipwrecks or on coral reefs. In two days they change into small starfish with arms. Now they can move about.

Did you know?

 A crown of thorns starfish is covered in prickly spines that cut attackers and leave them with nasty wounds.

 A crown of thorns starfish can have up to 23 arms. It can grow a new arm if one is bitten off or damaged.

 A starfish eats by pushing its stomach out through its mouth. The folds of the stomach wrap around the prey and digest it.

Crown of thorns starfish can live for eight years, but there is one predator that is not hurt by their spines...

Pufferfish

Pufferfish are slow swimmers, so they put off predators by blowing themselves up to look bigger than they are. If that fails, the poison in their bodies makes them a very nasty mouthful to eat.

1 When they mate, the male fish pushes the female up to the water's surface, where she lays her eggs. He fertilizes them as they float in the water.

2 The eggs hatch into larvae. Each larva has a bag of food, called a yolk sac, attached to its body. The food keeps it alive until it is able to catch prey.

Did you know?

When a pufferfish is scared, it fills its stretchy stomach with water until it is big and round like a balloon.

Pufferfish have hidden spines that stick up when the fish inflates. These make it difficult to swallow.

A pufferfish has a strong beak made of four teeth joined together.

4 Adult pufferfish can be 50 centimetres long. They live in warm waters and can survive for more than five years, eating starfish, crabs, fish and plants.

3 Over the next ten days the larvae grow into young fish, called fry. They can now feed themselves. As they grow they develop white spots and stripes on their skin.

A pufferfish's poison can kill, but some predators will eat it and take that risk...

Tiger shark

Tiger sharks are deadly hunters. They usually swim slowly and can get close to prey undetected. Then they put on a burst of speed and grab the prey before it can escape.

1 The female tiger shark mates with a male every three years. Up to 80 eggs develop into embryos in her womb, each with a yolk sac attached to its body.

2 After 16 months the shark gives birth to a litter of babies, called pups. They swim off and must look after themselves straight away.

Did you know?

When a shark attacks, eyelids cover its eyes to protect them from being damaged.

Some sharks have to swim all the time or they will drown. Swimming forces water through their gills so they can breathe.

A shark's jaws are lined with rows of sharp, triangular teeth. If one tooth breaks, another is ready to take its place.

4 It takes many years for sharks to reach adulthood. They can be 15 years old before they are able to mate.

3 Young tiger sharks have dark stripes on their bodies, which is how the fish gets its name. These markings fade as the sharks grow.

Tiger sharks are at the top of many food chains. No one knows for certain, but they may live for up to 40 years.

Pink shrimp

Pink shrimps are small, shelled sea animals. They live in the cold parts of the Pacific and the Atlantic oceans, eating tiny animals and plants. They in turn are food for many other animals in the ocean.

1 The female shrimp carries thousands of eggs on her rear legs until they hatch into larvae. Then she releases them.

2 The see-through larvae float freely in the water and start to eat algae.

Did you know?

Shrimps swim by flicking their tails forwards underneath their bodies. This pushes them backwards through the water.

They have two pairs of antennae, which they use to feel around for food or for danger.

Pink shrimps have ten pairs of legs. The front five pairs are for walking and feeding, the others are for swimming.

4 The juvenile shrimps are all males at this stage, but within a year they will change into females. When the sea temperature is right, they will lay their eggs and start the life cycle again.

3 After about four days the larvae change shape to become more like adult shrimps, although they are still see-through.

Pink shrimps can live for four years but only a few survive this long. Lots of other animals like to munch them up...

Black-eyed squid

Black-eyed squid are jet-propelled sea animals. Their bodies are like bags with eight arms and two longer tentacles which they use to reach out and grab their prey. They live mostly deep down in the ocean.

1 Most squid leave their eggs on the seabed, but the female black-eyed squid carries all 2000–3000 of them around with her in a sac as big as her body.

2 The eggs are held together in a special jelly. The female squid uses her arms to clean them and to keep the water moving around them.

4 As the babies leave to feed and grow into adults, the female squid is so tired and hungry that she dies.

3 It takes 6—9 months for the eggs to hatch. During this time, the female squid stays with them and does not eat.

Did you know?

Squid confuse attackers by shooting a cloud of dark ink into their eyes. This gives the squid a chance to escape.

A squid's eyes face in opposite directions. This gives it good all-round vision.

A squid's arms and tentacles are covered with suckers which it uses to grab prey and pull it into its mouth.

Black-eyed squid can live for two years, but many are snapped up by other animals before then...

Silver salmon

Silver salmon spend part of their lives in the ocean. Then they go on an amazing journey, swimming upriver to return to the place where they were born.

1 The female digs a nest in the gravel bed of a stream. She lays thousands of eggs, which are fertilized by males, and then she covers them up. She does this a few times. The eggs hatch after several months.

2 The hatchlings stay in the nest for up to two weeks. They hardly move and live on their yolk sacs — bags of food attached to their bodies.

4 Adult silver salmon stay at sea for between one and three years. Then they swim back to where they were born. Not even waterfalls will stop them. Once there, they mate, lay their eggs and die.

3 The hatchlings grow into young fish, and start to eat tiny insects and plants. They will live in fresh water for about a year before they swim downriver to the salty sea.

 A salmon is shaped like a rocket to move smoothly through the water. Its eight fins help it balance and turn.

 Some experts believe that salmon use their sense of smell to find their way back to the river where they were born.

 Silver salmon develop bright red sides when they swim into fresh water.

Very few salmon complete their incredible journey. There are many predators in the water, and also in the air...

19

Bald eagle

Bald eagles are huge birds of prey with sharp talons and hooked beaks. They glide over seas and rivers, swooping down to grab fish.

1 Bald eagles mate for life. They build nests high in tall trees, on cliffs near the coast or beside rivers, and expand them each year.

2 Females lay up to three eggs and the parents take it in turns to guard the nest. They sit on the eggs to keep them warm for about 35 days.

Did you know?

Eagles see five times better than humans. They are able to spot a fish in shallow water 1.6 kilometres away.

Eagles lift fish out of the water in their strong, sharp talons. They hold it with one foot and tear it apart with their beaks.

If a bald eagle catches a fish that it cannot lift, it paddles to the shore using its wings.

4 The young eagles first start to fly when they are about 12 weeks old, but they live in the nest for another eight weeks while they learn how to hunt.

3 Then the chicks hatch. They are too weak to stand up until they are 4–5 weeks old. They are always hungry and open their big beaks every time a parent returns to the nest.

Bald eagles are so big and fierce that they are at the top of many food chains. They live for about 30 years.

Box jellyfish

Box jellyfish look like harmless blobs but their tentacles carry a powerful sting for catching prey. They swim through tropical waters eating crustaceans and fish.

1 The females release their eggs into shallow water near the coast. The males fertilize the eggs.

2 Tiny larvae hatch out and sink down until they land on a surface like a rock or the seabed. Here they develop into polyps with tentacles.

4 The polyps grow into tiny jellyfish, called medusas. They leave the seabed and float away to feed until they become adults and are ready to breed.

3 The polyps trap prey in their tentacles. Over many months the polyps grow buds and more new polyps grow out of the buds. Soon there is a small colony of polyps.

Did you know?

Box jellyfish have four sets of tentacles. Each one of these tentacles has 500,000 poisonous stinging cells.

Unlike other jellyfish, box jellyfish swim well and steer towards the light. Other jellyfish simply drift.

A jellyfish has one opening underneath its umbrella-like bell. Food comes in and waste goes out through it.

Box jellyfish live for about a year. They are attacked by larger animals that are not harmed by their poisonous stings...

Sea turtle

Loggerhead turtles are champion divers: they can stay underwater for up to four hours. They paddle the oceans, feeding on plants and other animals, including jellyfish.

1 At night the female comes to the flat, sandy beach where she was born. She lays about 100 eggs and covers them up. She does this about four times in each mating season.

2 The babies grow inside the eggs for about 80 days. Then they break out of the shells using a special sharp egg tooth which they lose afterwards.

Did you know?

Turtles have no teeth. Instead they have beak-like mouths and spines in their throats to stop their prey escaping.

Turtles pull themselves through the water with their long front flippers and use the back ones to steer.

A turtle's red-brown shell is called a carapace. Sometimes small animals, such as barnacles, live on it.

4 When they are more than 17 years old, the adult females return to the same beach to lay their eggs. They will do this every 2—3 years. The males never come ashore again.

3 The hatchlings look for the bright light of the moon shining on the sea and crawl across the sand towards it. Then they swim out to sea.

Loggerhead turtles can live for 50 years. They are so big that only animals with large mouths can attack them...

Orca

Orcas, or killer whales, are sometimes called the 'wolves of the sea' because they hunt in packs. They eat anything they can catch, including sea turtles.

1 Orcas mate every five years and the females have one baby at a time. The baby grows inside its mother's womb for 15–18 months.

2 A baby orca, or calf, is born with black and yellow skin. It gradually sheds this skin and the yellow areas change to white.

Did you know?

The dorsal fin helps the orca turn and stay upright. A male's dorsal fin can be 2 metres high.

4 Orcas live in groups called pods. Calves remain with their pod for years; female calves stay forever. A pod might have a grandmother, her daughter and her daughter's calves in it.

Orcas have between 40 and 56 teeth. Each tooth is 7.5 centimetres long and curved to help it grip prey.

3 Like all mammal babies, an orca calf needs its mother's milk. It feeds several times an hour, 24 hours a day, for a year.

Orcas breathe air through a blowhole in the top of their heads. When they dive, a flap stops water getting in.

Orcas live for about 50 years. No other animal attacks them, so they are at the top of many food chains.

An Atlantic food web

This book follows three ocean food chains.
Most animals eat more than one food, however,
so they are part of many food chains. There are
lots of food chains in an ocean,
and they link up like a map
to make a food web.

Sailfish

Gull

Orca

Sea turtle

Shark

Crab

Jellyfish

Clam

Plankton

Sun

Mackerel

Seahorse

This is a food web from the Atlantic ocean.

Glossary

ALGAE
Plant-like living things that make their food using the sun's energy.

ANTENNAE
A pair of feelers on a shrimp's head.

CARNIVORE
An animal that eats other animals.

CONSUMER
A living thing that survives by eating other living things.

CRUSTACEAN
A group of animals that includes shrimps and crabs. They have three main body parts and an external skeleton.

DIGEST
When the body breaks down food to get the nutrients, or goodness, that will keep it alive.

EMBRYO
An early form of a baby animal growing inside its mother.

FERTILIZE
When sperm from a male animal meets the egg of a female to make a new life.

FIN
Part of a fish's body that helps it to balance and steer through the water.

FRESH WATER
Water that is not salty like seawater.

GILLS
The organs used to breathe underwater.

HATCHLING
An animal just born from a hard-shelled egg.

INFLATE
To fill with air or water.

JUVENILE
Another word for young.

LARVA
A young animal that will change its body shape to become an adult. Groups are called larvae.

MATE
When a male and female animal reproduce. For some animals there is a particular time each year when they mate and this is called the 'mating season'.

OMNIVORE
An animal that eats plants and other animals.

PLANKTON
Tiny living things that drift in seas and oceans. If they are plants, they are called phytoplankton. If they are animals, they are called zooplankton.

POD
A group of whales.

POISON
A substance that harms living things.

POLYP
An animal with a soft body and a mouth surrounded by tentacles.

PREDATOR
An animal that kills and eats other animals.

PREY
An animal hunted by a predator.

PRODUCER
A living thing that makes its own food from the energy of the sun.

SAC
A bag of food attached to a baby animal, or a bag of eggs (see the black-eyed squid).

SPAWNING
When sea animals release their eggs to be fertilized.

SUCKER
A cup-shaped part of an animal's arm, used for gripping things.

TALON
A bird's claw.

TENTACLE
A long, thin arm usually used for gripping and feeding.

TROPICAL
Seas around the Equator where the water is warmer because it gets the most sunshine.

WOMB
The part of a female animal where babies grow.

YOLK
The goodness inside an egg which feeds a new baby animal.

These websites have information about oceans, or their animals, or both!

- ocean.nationalgeographic.com/ocean
- animaldiversity.ummz.umich.edu/site/index.html
- arkive.org/education
- bbc.co.uk/nature/blueplanet
- earthskids.com/ek_science-marine.htm
- enchantedlearning.com/subjects/ocean
- thekidswindow.co.uk/News/Oceans_Quiz.htm
- iiseagrant.org/NabInvader

Index